ANXIETY
Calming the Fearful Heart

JUNE HUNT

AspirePress

Anxiety: Calming the Fearful Heart
©2021 Hope For The Heart

Published by Aspire Press
An imprint of Hendrickson Publishing Group
Rose Publishing, LLC
P.O. Box 3473
Peabody, Massachusetts 01961-3473 USA
www.HendricksonPublishingGroup.com

ISBN 9781628629859

The views and opinions expressed in this book are those of the author(s) and do not necessarily express the views of Rose Publishing, LLC, nor is this book intended to be a substitute for mental health treatment or professional counseling. The information in this resource is intended as guidelines for healthy living. Please consult qualified medical, legal, pastoral, and psychological professionals regarding individual concerns.

Cover photo: biletskiyevgeniy.com/Shutterstock.com

Unless otherwise indicated, all Scripture quotations are taken from the Holy Bible, New International Version®, NIV®. Copyright © 1973, 1978, 1984, 2011 by Biblica, Inc.™ Used by permission of Zondervan. All rights reserved worldwide. www.zondervan.com The "NIV" and "New International Version" are trademarks registered in the United States Patent and Trademark Office by Biblica, Inc.™ Scripture quotations marked (NKJV) are taken from the New King James Version®. Copyright © 1982 by Thomas Nelson. Used by permission. All rights reserved. Scripture quotations marked (NLT) are taken from the Holy Bible, New Living Translation, copyright © 1996, 2004, 2015 by Tyndale House Foundation. Used by permission of Tyndale House Publishers, Inc., Carol Stream, Illinois 60188. All rights reserved. Scripture quotations marked (ESV) are taken from The ESV® Bible (The Holy Bible, English Standard Version®), copyright © 2001 by Crossway, a publishing ministry of Good News Publishers. Used by permission. All rights reserved. Scripture quotations marked (CEV) are from the Contemporary English Version Copyright © 1991, 1992, 1995 by American Bible Society. Used by Permission. Scripture quotations marked (NASB) taken from the New American Standard Bible® (NASB), Copyright © 1960, 1962, 1963, 1968, 1971, 1972, 1973, 1975, 1977, 1995 by The Lockman Foundation Used by permission. www.Lockman.org. Scripture quotations marked (MSG) are taken from THE MESSAGE, copyright © 1993, 2002, 2018 by Eugene H. Peterson. Used by permission of NavPress. All rights reserved. Represented by Tyndale House Publishers, a Division of Tyndale House Ministries.

For more information on Hope For The Heart, visit www.hopefortheheart.org or call 1-800-488-HOPE (4673).

Printed in the United States of America
020221VP

CONTENTS

Dear friend,

How well I remember helping my friend Elizabeth in her struggle with fear and anxiety.

Several years ago, we were working on an article together for the ministry. As we discussed the topic of fear related to the piece, she revealed that she was mortally afraid of the dark.

"Oh, Elizabeth, how difficult that must be," I replied. I felt honored to be trusted with something so personal. I told her I'd like to know more if she was willing to share. After working closely together for years, we trusted each other and she agreed to discuss this issue.

First I asked, "When is the first time you can recall being afraid in the dark? What were the circumstances?"

"I don't know. Nothing comes to … *Wait!*" she said. Suddenly, a long-submerged memory materialized in that moment and she began telling me about an event that happened to her when she was just seven years old. Her three older siblings took some thread and suspended her doll in the middle of a dark bedroom. Then they flicked the light on and off like a strobe light to make it look like Thumbelina was floating in mid-air. "She's been captured by evil fairies and you're the only one who can save her," they announced. She lunged toward the doll—and off went the lights. Ensnared in a tangled web of thread, she cried for help but was ignored. She felt trapped and terrified.

Realize, the past affects our present a great deal. I can think of numerous cases in my own life and in the lives of others where painful memories, past abuse, or traumatic experiences have led to fear and anxiety in the present. Understandably, these are multifaceted, complex emotions and experiences—but for Elizabeth, I could see the connection between this memory and her present fear and anxiety about being in dark places.

Thankfully, no matter what has happened in our past, the Lord can help us in the present and give us hope for the future.

After listening to Elizabeth, I tried to help her apply God's Word to her situation. I shared Psalm 56:3, which says, "*Whenever I am afraid, I will trust in You*" (NKJV).

I said, "Notice this verse doesn't say, 'if,' but '*when* I am afraid.' At times, both you and I *will* have fear and anxiety. It's undeniable. However, we don't have to be consumed by them."

Then, I suggested an exercise for her: "Every time you enter a dark room and feel anxious, say Psalm 56:3 *out loud*. Think about each word as you say it. Say it over and over, as many times as you need, until you feel your peace returning. I want you to speak God's Word over your fear and anxiety."

Elizabeth tried this exercise for about ten days—and was amazed at the results. She said, "I can't even say for sure when it began to happen—or how—but, little by little, my fear of the dark is fading away. I've been saying Psalm 56:3 every time fear and anxiety begin welling up inside me. At first, I felt a little silly, talking aloud alone in my apartment. But, honestly, it's amazing how saying that one simple scripture has had such an impact. The fear is losing its grip!"

What a blessing to see God's Word at work! Even for a complex issue like anxiety which can affect many dimensions in our lives—our emotions, our bodies, our relationships, and of course, our minds—the Lord can speak into it. That's why I meet fearful, anxious thoughts with the truth of God's Word. I've learned this valuable lesson:

> *Focus on your fear,*
> *and your panic will increase.*
> *Focus on your Shepherd,*
> *and your heart will be at peace.*

The Lord wants to give you His peace when you're feeling anxious. I pray that as you seek Him when facing any situation that causes you fear, worry, or anxiety, you will experience His peace—a peace that "*surpasses all understanding*" (Philippians 4:7 ESV).

Hold on to the Lord's promise: "*You will keep in perfect peace all who trust in you, all whose thoughts are fixed on you!*" (Isaiah 26:3 NLT).

Yours in the Lord's hope,

June Hunt

ANXIETY
Calming the Fearful Heart

You see it in the little toddler as Mommy drops her off at day care or in a student who's always silent, afraid to speak in class. You see it in the child who's waiting for a flu shot or a patient who's waiting on test results. You see it in a speaker who hesitantly stands up to give a presentation or in a fearful friend who repeatedly declines your invitation to see a movie or go to a party.

You *see* it in the shaky hands, tapping feet, tense shoulders, or endless pacing of a loved one. You *hear* it in the short breaths, constant questions, irritable tone, and irrational fears expressed by a neighbor. You may *feel* it yourself—the pounding heart, the sweaty palms, the abdominal pain, the pressure in your chest, even hot flashes and cold chills. Then there's the mental impact of racing thoughts, trouble concentrating, wide-eyed insomnia, persistent nightmares, or fearful unknowns accompanied by the ongoing stress and strain in your mind and in your body. What is it?

Anxiety!

For some, anxiety comes and goes as a temporary visitor that occupies only one small space of life. For others, anxiety makes itself right at home. It's a lifelong guest that settles into every area of your life, constantly disrupting your day and affecting your loved ones.

Whether anxiety is a temporary visitor or a lifelong lodger, you also have a constant companion—a faithful friend—who promises never to leave you. He is your strong Savior who walks beside you every day, helping and upholding you each step of the way. He is the Lord. And He says these words to calm your anxious heart ...

"Do not fear, for I am with you;
do not be dismayed, for I am your God.
I will strengthen you and help you;
I will uphold you
with my righteous right hand."
Isaiah 41:10

DEFINITIONS

We live life on the run. Under constant stress and unyielding strain, most people today live at too fast of a pace. Adrenaline has become our "high-octane" energy source of choice as we live increasingly hurried, hassled, and harried lives. The pace at which we live stretches us beyond our limits, and we pay a high price in the form of stress and anxiety.

In fact, did you know that anxiety is the number one mental health problem among American women, and is second only to alcohol and drug abuse in men?[1] And an estimated 264 million people worldwide experienced an anxiety disorder in 2017, making it the most prevalent mental health disorder around the globe.[2]

For many, anxiety is equally debilitating and destructive, beyond the reach of a peaceful balance. But anxiety is much more than an isolated response to the troubles of our time. Anxiety invades unexpectedly to grasp a person's heart and mind, amplifying fear and imprisoning people in its frightening grip.

For those caught in this emotional snare, the Lord offers help and hope to calm anxious hearts.

> "Be strong and take heart,
> all you who hope in the LORD."
> Psalm 31:24

You're driving to work one day when the thought crosses your mind, *Did I close the garage door?* You begin to mentally retrace your steps, but don't recall with any degree of certainty that you actually *did* close it. You probably did, but what if you didn't? You feel the anxiety beginning to build as you imagine someone walking into your open house and stealing anything and everything of value to you. Just then, the car to your right starts to drift into your lane. You clutch the steering wheel tightly, lay on your horn, and hit your brakes to avoid being sideswiped. A surge of adrenaline pulses through your body putting you on high alert. Your heart is pounding, your mind is racing, your palms are sweating … but you're okay. You take a deep breath and heave a sigh of relief as you think, *Whew, that was close!*

Anxiety is a normal part of life. It goes with being human and living in our high-stress world. Normal anxiety keeps us busy. It reminds us to pay our bills and pushes us to pursue success. In its pure form, anxiety can serve a useful purpose, but anxiety is only normal up to a point. As long as anxious feelings are short-lived and don't become excessive, they won't interfere with healthy living. However, anxiety becomes destructive when it throws you into a state of distress and weighs you down, sometimes to such a degree that you cannot function normally. Proverbs accurately presents the weightiness of anxiety …

"Anxiety weighs down the heart."
Proverbs 12:25

▶ **Anxiety** is a feeling of nervous apprehension usually over something imminent which has an uncertain outcome, affecting a person both physically and psychologically.[3]

▶ **Anxiety** has its roots in the ancient Greek word *angh*:[4]

- The Greeks used this word to express the idea of being burdened or troubled (for example, *angh*uished).

- It was used primarily in reference to physical sensations such as tightness, constriction, or discomfort. Angina is a medical condition in which chest pains occur because of heart disease. The word *angina* comes from the word *angh*.[5]

▶ *Anxious* in New Testament Greek is *merimnao*, meaning "to be anxious about, to have a distracting care."[6]

- The same Greek word is used for *worry*, literally meaning "to have a divided mind."

- *Merimna* means "to draw in different directions, to distract." Thus the warning in Luke 21:34: *"Be careful, or your hearts will be weighed down with ... the anxieties of life."*

▶ **Anxiety** stems from uncertainty and, therefore, is an uneasiness over an uncertain outcome.

- Hoping something will happen, but having no guarantee that it will.

- Fearing something will happen, but having no assurance that it won't.

▶ **Anxiety** reflects an excessively negative presumption:

- Overestimating the probability of danger
- Overexaggerating the "terribleness" of something

▶ **Anxiety Disorders** are intense, excessive feelings of helplessness and dread, even when the threat of danger is mild or nonexistent.

- Disorders impair normal functioning or the normal living of life.
- Disorder sufferers organize their lives around attempts to avoid anxiety.

In the Bible, when the Israelites find themselves in captivity, they are described as having ...

> " ... an anxious mind, eyes weary with longing, and a despairing heart."
> Deuteronomy 28:65

WHAT ARE Anxiety Disorders?

The National Institute of Mental Health explains anxiety disorders in this way:

Occasional anxiety is an expected part of life. You might feel anxious when faced with a problem at work, before taking a test, or before making an important decision. But anxiety disorders involve more than temporary worry or fear. For a person with an anxiety disorder, the anxiety does not go away and can get worse over time. The symptoms can interfere with daily activities such as job performance, schoolwork, and relationships.[7]

Several types of anxiety disorders exist that disrupt daily routines (at home, work, or school), including generalized anxiety disorder, panic disorder, and various phobia-related disorders. Anxiety evolves into a disorder when it becomes so intense that it takes over a person's thoughts, feelings and actions, preventing the anxiety-controlled person from living a normal life. Generally, those who experience an anxiety disorder feel isolated, alone, and different—like the only one in the world trapped by "this terrible thing." Obviously, there is a reason. But the Bible says ...

"Do not be anxious about anything,
but in every situation,
by prayer and petition,
with thanksgiving,
present your requests to God."
Philippians 4:6

Most Common Anxiety Disorders

▶ **Generalized Anxiety Disorder (GAD)**—An ongoing state of worry, concern, and heightened anxiety over everyday events for six months or more.[8]

- Generalized Anxiety Disorder is excessive worry about *what if*, *what might*, and *what could* happen with no discernible solution, no end, and no peace.

- Generalized Anxiety Disorder sufferers worry about everyday things every day. They know they worry too much but just can't seem to control their thoughts.

14

- Generalized Anxiety Disorder is accompanied by at least three of the following symptoms:
  - ▶ Feeling tired for no reason
  - ▶ Having trouble falling or staying asleep
  - ▶ Startling easily
  - ▶ Unable to relax for any length of time
  - ▶ Experiencing muscle tension and aches
  - ▶ Trembling or twitching
  - ▶ Being irritable
  - ▶ Having difficulty concentrating

▶ **Panic Disorder**—Sudden and repeated attacks of overwhelming fear with physical symptoms lasting several minutes or longer.[9]

- Panic Attacks are extraordinary episodes of terror over nothing discernible. They become a "disorder" when the problem persists longer than a month.

- Panic Disorders sometimes run in families and often begin in the late teens or early adulthood.[10]

- Panic Disorders are characterized by these symptoms:
  - ▶ Fearing death or having a sense of impending doom
  - ▶ Pounding or racing heart, sweating, breathing problems, tingly or numb hands, chest pain
  - ▶ Fearing when the next panic attack will happen

▶ Feeling out of control

▶ Fearing going to places where prior panic attacks have occurred

▶ **Specific Phobias**—Persistent, marked irrational fear of an object or situation that leads to the avoidance of that object or situation.[11]

- Phobias must be an excessive and incapacitating fear to be considered a phobia.

- Phobias can trigger a severe anxiety reaction or even a panic attack.

- Specific phobias are varied and diverse. Some include:

  ▶ Agoraphobia—fear of crowds, open area, or public spaces (literally, fear of the marketplace)

  ▶ Aviophobia—fear of flying

  ▶ Bacillophobia—fear of germs

  ▶ Coulrophobia—fear of clowns

  ▶ Cynophobia—fear of dogs

  ▶ Nomophobia—fear of being alone

▶ **Social Anxiety Disorder** (also called *social phobia*)—An intense, persistent fear of being watched, judged, or humiliated by others.[12]

- Social Anxiety Disorder is a common type of anxiety disorder. Symptoms of this disorder must exist for at least six months and make it difficult for someone to do everyday tasks. Someone with this disorder is anxious or fearful in certain or all social situations (for example, meeting new people, dating, eating or drinking in front of others, using a public restroom). The underlying fear driving this disorder is that of being judged or humiliated.

- Social Anxiety Disorder may reveal itself as *performance anxiety* when in social situations (for example, giving a speech, singing, dancing or playing a musical instrument on stage).

- Social Anxiety Disorder presents with these signs and symptoms:

  ▶ Blushing, sweating, trembling, feeling as if your mind is "going blank"

  ▶ Feeling sick to your stomach

  ▶ Making little eye contact or speaking with an overly soft voice

  ▶ Being self-conscious in front of other people

  ▶ Feeling embarrassed and awkward

  ▶ Having difficulty talking to people you don't know even when you wish you could

Anxiety can leave its victims feeling as unsettled as Job ...

> "I have no peace, no quietness;
> I have no rest, but only turmoil."
> Job 3:26

QUESTION: "Is there a difference between an anxiety attack and a panic attack?"

ANSWER: Yes. Although there are differences, there are also some similarities.

▶ **Differences**—Perhaps the most distinctive difference has to do with the suddenness of the feelings. Someone having an anxiety attack tends to maintain a low level of anxiety most of the time. The anxiousness builds but eventually settles down again to a normal level. With anxiety attacks you can't just snap out of feeling the way you do. Someone who has a panic attack will generally feel fine before it happens and symptoms typically go away within thirty to sixty minutes. Symptoms are unprovoked and unpredictable, but they quickly end on their own, leaving the sufferer feeling exhausted and spent.

▶ **Similarities**—Both anxiety attacks and panic attacks activate the fight, flight, or freeze reaction in the body where the sympathetic nervous system triggers the brain to release hormones that rev up the body. Two symptoms common to both anxiety and panic attacks are shallow breathing and trouble thinking. Both symptoms can be exacerbated by worrying about them. There is no real risk or actual danger in either scenario—it only feels like there is.

Treatment of these anxiety problems will likely differ, so check with a medical physician to determine both the cause and the cure for any attacks you may have as well as calling out to the Lord for help and healing.

QUESTION: "What is the connection between stress, anxiety, and depression?"

ANSWER: Stress that goes on for too long or becomes chronic can lead to anxiety. Intense anxiety can impact brain (and body) chemistry, which in turn can lead to the onset of depression. Many people with anxiety also develop depression and vice versa. Each of these mental health conditions manifest in different ways.

▶ **Stress** is how the brain and body respond to any demand.

- All different types of stress carry physical and mental health risks.

- A stressor can be a one-time or short-term occurrence, or it can be an occurrence that keeps happening over a long period of time.

- Not all stress is bad. Healthy stress can motivate people to prepare or to perform. It becomes unhealthy when the stress response goes beyond physical, mental, and emotional limits resulting in distress, danger, and destruction.

- Routine stress, called *eustress*, is probably the most difficult to notice. If this type of stress goes from being constant to acute, eventually it will cause the body to no longer get a clear signal to return to normal functioning. This can contribute to serious health problems such as heart disease, high blood pressure, and diabetes, as well as mental health conditions like anxiety and depression.

▶ **Anxiety** is a reaction to stress and often comes from a place of fear, unease, and worry.

- While there is a definite overlap between the two, anxiety and stress have different origins. With stress, you know what's worrying you. With anxiety, you tend not to be aware of what is actually making you anxious.

- The terms *anxiety* and *stress* are often used interchangeably, but they're different experiences. Stress is associated with frustration and nervousness, whereas anxiety is more of an emotional reaction that *becomes* a problem.

- Anxiety and stressful situations can produce similar physical and mental symptoms such as stomach problems, muscle tension, rapid breathing, change in appetite, and trouble sleeping.

- Anxiety and stress that occur frequently or seem out of proportion to the stressor may be signs of an anxiety disorder and should be evaluated by a doctor.

▶ **Depression** is a common but serious mood disorder that causes severe symptoms affecting how someone thinks, feels, and handles daily activities.[14]

- Characteristically, someone struggling with depression generally lacks interest in enjoyable activities, experiences an increase or decrease in appetite, has low energy, trouble concentrating, and often feels worthless.

- To be diagnosed with depression, five or more symptoms must be present for at least two weeks.

- What distinguishes depression from anxiety is that a person who is depressed tends to move slowly and his or her reactions can seem flattened or dulled, whereas someone with anxiety is more likely to be keyed up and struggles to manage racing thoughts.

- Many people who develop depression have a history of an anxiety disorder earlier in life. No evidence proves one disorder causes the other, but there is clear evidence that many people suffer from both disorders.[15]

Remember this: *God rescues all who are discouraged and gives them hope.*

"The LORD is there
to rescue all who are discouraged
and have given up hope."
Psalm 34:18 CEV

Anxiety inaccurately judges reality. It forgets the past and fears the future. It fails to remember how you've made it through past difficulties and focuses instead on potential threats in the future. Anxiety leaves you with a fight or flight response in the present, vigilantly preparing for possible outcomes or avoiding fearful situations altogether.

The Lord, however, sees all things clearly. He says, *"I make known the end from the beginning, from ancient times, what is still to come. I say, 'My purpose will stand, and I will do all that I please'"* (Isaiah 46:10).

God has brought you through the past and holds your future in His hands. And in your present struggle with anxiety, He is with you. The Lord is at work in your life. Your anxiety is not without purpose. God longs to be your refuge and help you walk through your fears and troubles.

> "God is our refuge and strength,
> an ever-present help in trouble."
> Psalm 46:1

1. **God wants you to remember that He is good and gracious—and compassionately cares about you.**

   "The LORD is gracious and compassionate, slow to anger and rich in love. The LORD is good to all; he has compassion on all he has made" (Psalm 145:8–9).

2. **God wants you to remember He is with you when you're fearful.**

   "So do not fear, for I am with you; do not be dismayed, for I am your God. I will strengthen you and help you; I will uphold you with my righteous right hand" (Isaiah 41:10).

3. **God wants you to pray and experience His peace when you're feeling anxious.**

   "Do not be anxious about anything, but in every situation, by prayer and petition, with thanksgiving, present your requests to God. And the peace of God, which transcends all understanding, will guard your hearts and your minds in Christ Jesus" (Philippians 4:6–7).

4. **God wants you to look to Him and His Word when you're filled with anxiety.**

   "When anxiety was great within me, your consolation brought me joy" (Psalm 94:19).

5. **God wants you to align your thoughts with His truth when you feel anxious.**

   "Whatever is true, whatever is noble, whatever is right, whatever is pure, whatever is lovely, whatever is admirable—if anything is excellent or praiseworthy— think about such things" (Philippians 4:8).

6. **God wants you to trust Him when you're anxious—to have faith and not fear.**

   "When I am afraid, I put my trust in you" (Psalm 56:3).

7. **God wants you to talk to Him about all that causes you to feel anxious.**

   "Cast all your anxiety on him because he cares for you" (1 Peter 5:7).

8. **God wants you to talk to others about your fears and anxieties.**

   "Where there is no guidance the people fall, But in abundance of counselors there is victory" (Proverbs 11:14 NASB).

9. **God wants you to take care of yourself physically and spiritually.**

   "For physical training is of some value, but godliness has value for all things, holding promise for both the present life and the life to come" (1 Timothy 4:8).

10. **God wants you to encourage others who struggle with anxiety.**

    "Anxiety weighs down the heart, but a kind word cheers it up" (Proverbs 12:25).

CHARACTERISTICS

Picture an intelligent person, someone who exhibits kindness and compassion. Known to be extremely responsible, this person does a good job well (might even be a bit of a perfectionist).

Now imagine the same person in what most people might consider a mildly fearful situation. You see an individual who remains hypervigilant, yet is easily startled. Making a decision on what to do next seems like an insurmountable obstacle. Negative thoughts intrude, then panic and paralysis take over. On the outside, this person who appears calm, cool, and collected is strenuously struggling with anxiety within.

The prophet Isaiah spoke of such internal turmoil ...

> "My mind reels and my heart races.
> I longed for evening to come,
> but now I am terrified of the dark."
> Isaiah 21:4 NLT

But these words in Scripture reassure ...

> "Let the beloved of the LORD rest secure
> in him, for he shields him all day long,
> and the one the LORD loves rests
> between his shoulders."
> Deuteronomy 33:12

Few people want to admit they struggle with anxiety. Many dedicated and conscientious people who appear to "have it all together" discover they, too, are susceptible to becoming overworked and overwhelmed. When adrenaline infuses the body, the surge of energy can seem productive, but that same exhilaration that serves to fuel a "fight or flight" (and sometimes "freeze") response in an emergency can also mask signs of overstress. In such cases, a seemingly "out of nowhere" panic attack could be a warning that anxiety is building and needs to be addressed.

The Bible recounts David's plea for relief ...

"Give me relief from my distress;
have mercy on me and hear my prayer. ...
Fill my heart with joy ...
In peace I will lie down and sleep for you
alone, LORD, make me dwell in safety."
Psalm 4:1, 7–8

Review the following lists of symptoms. If you experience at least three symptoms in each category, anxiety might be developing into a problem, especially if occurring frequently. If you experience more than three symptoms from each category, consult a physician without delay.

An Anxiety Assessment

Behavioral Symptoms

- ❏ Decision-making impaired
- ❏ Irritability
- ❏ Fidgety
- ❏ Jumpy, "on edge"
- ❏ Heavy sighs
- ❏ Overly talkative
- ❏ Hyperalert
- ❏ Quivering voice
- ❏ Hyperventilation, dizziness, or fainting
- ❏ Sleep difficulties

Cognitive Symptoms

You think ...

- ❏ "I can't go on like this."
- ❏ "I must be going crazy."
- ❏ "I've got to escape and get out of here."
- ❏ "I'm all alone and I can't make it without help."
- ❏ "I might make a fool of myself!"
- ❏ "I can't go out because I'll lose control."
- ❏ "I must be having a heart attack."
- ❏ "People are always watching me."
- ❏ "I feel like I'm going to faint."
- ❏ "I can't remember things and that scares me."

Emotional Symptoms

You feel …

- ❏ "I feel consumed with fear."
- ❏ "I feel isolated from others."
- ❏ "I feel so uneasy."
- ❏ "I feel rejected."
- ❏ "I feel alone—and lonely."
- ❏ "I feel deeply depressed."
- ❏ "I feel embarrassed."
- ❏ "I feel I've lost control."
- ❏ "I'm angry and want to scream."
- ❏ "I'm terrified something bad will happen."

Physical Symptoms

- ❏ Abdominal pain, diarrhea, or nausea
- ❏ Impaired concentration
- ❏ Butterflies in the stomach
- ❏ Memory disturbance
- ❏ Clammy hands
- ❏ Muscle tension, trembling, or twitching
- ❏ Excessive perspiration
- ❏ Rapid heartbeat
- ❏ Headaches
- ❏ Ulcers

Some small measure of anxiety is normal—and can even be considered beneficial. Such anxiety registers as *concern*, which works toward finding a solution to the concern. On the contrary, increased frequent anxiety can become intrusive, and overwhelming anxiety can be detrimental. Much like running on a hamster wheel, energy is expended but you don't go anywhere.

Of course, we can experience high levels of anxiety when we perceive the situation we're in to be precarious. In fact, many people find themselves walking the tightrope from tension to terror, from unrest to extreme fear.

When we find ourselves walking that tense tightrope, if we turn our focus from our fears to the Lord, we move toward walking in the Spirit—walking with peace and calm with Him. We can then say with assurance ...

"Though I walk in the midst of trouble,
you preserve my life.
You stretch out your hand
against the anger of my foes;
with your right hand you save me."
Psalm 138:7

ANXIETY CONTINUUM

Normal	Mild to Moderate	Intense

Anxiety ranges from normally mild and can increase to moderate, and from severe to severely debilitating. Depending on the type of anxiety experienced, it can stay at a manageable level or reach an intensity so tremendous, it interferes with daily life and makes living moment-to-moment a struggle.

We all experience times of anxiety—times of tension—but not all of us experience it in the same way, or for the same reason, or to the same degree. It can be a friend or foe. Typically, we want to avoid it. However, anxiety is not to be feared, but to be understood and managed as you trust in the Lord. To the trouble-hearted, Jesus said …

> "Do not let your hearts be troubled.
> You believe in God; believe also in me."
> John 14:1

▶ **Normal anxiety** can be healthy and helpful when …

- It motivates and leads to increased efficiency.

- It forces you out of your comfort zone.

- It helps you avoid dangerous situations.

- It causes you to live dependently on the Lord.

▶ **Mild to moderate anxiety** becomes limiting, impedes daily routines, and begins to interfere with daily living when …

- It makes concentration difficult.

- It causes forgetfulness.

- It hinders performance.

- It blocks communication with others.

▶ **Intense anxiety**, an abnormal fearful obsession, is more profound and problematic when …

- It becomes a severe preoccupation with your fears.

- It requires tremendous effort to avoid triggers.

- It impacts your physical health to an alarming degree.

- It harms your relationships in many areas—professionally and personally.

> "When anxiety was great within me,
> your consolation brought me joy."
> Psalm 94:19

Worry and Anxiety

QUESTION: "What is the difference between worry and anxiety?"

ANSWER: People often use the words *worry* and *anxiety* interchangeably. However, there are key differences between the two:

▶ **Worry** is typically understood to be a *mental* process—ruminating on what-if scenarios that may or may not come to fruition in the future. It is often anticipating an outcome, attempting to solve a problem or avoiding a deeper issue. Worry is not an emotion or a feeling—like joy, anger, or love. However, worry can reveal hidden fear. Although worry is not an emotion, it can lead to feeling anxious.

▶ **Anxiety** is a present physiological feeling, usually an emotional response to a current or possible future threat (real or perceived). Anxiety becomes problematic when it is excessive or persistent (with individual episodes extending six months or more), known as Generalized Anxiety Disorder (GAD).[17] Excessive, obsessive worry can *lead* to anxiety. Likewise, stress can lead to worry or anxiety. Anxiety can also make an appearance all on its own.

DIFFERENCES BETWEEN WORRY AND ANXIETY[18]

WORRY	ANXIETY
Experienced through thoughts in the mind	Experienced throughout the body
Specific object of worry	Can be specific, but often is not
Most often is expressed verbally in the mind (thoughts)	More emotional (images); felt throughout the body
Focused on linear problem solving (in search of strategies to find a solution)	Focus is more cyclical (like being on a hamster wheel)
Rarely interferes with daily living	Can disrupt personal and professional function

WORRY	ANXIETY
Often related to more realistic concerns	Often based on unlikely occurrences
Can usually be controllable	More difficult to control
Can be alleviated and dismissed once an issue is resolved	Can linger for long periods of time and progress into other issues
Generally causes mild emotional distress	Can create severe emotional distress
Usually considered a "normal" psychological state	Can be considered a disorder requiring treatment depending on intensity and duration

Anxious Christian

QUESTION: "I am anxious all the time. Does my anxiety mean I'm not a good Christian?"

ANSWER: No. God doesn't qualify or quantify your status as a Christian by comparing you with others. You may experience anxiety at the thought of speaking in public or face an irrational fear of snow even if you live in a desert, but God doesn't expect everyone to have the boldness of Daniel facing the lions' den or his three friends entering the fiery furnace. Can you imagine the anxious dread they may have felt? Even Jesus was *"deeply distressed and troubled … overwhelmed with sorrow"* as he was praying in the garden of Gethsemane before His arrest and betrayal leading to His death on the cross (see Mark 14:33–34).

Feeling anxious doesn't make you an inferior Christian. It simply means you are human.[19]

Remember, the Bible says …

> "May God himself, the God of peace,
> sanctify you through and through.
> May your whole spirit, soul and body
> be kept blameless at the coming
> of our Lord Jesus Christ.
> The one who calls you is faithful,
> and he will do it."
> 1 Thessalonians 5:23–24

WHAT ARE Myths and Misconceptions about Anxiety?

Why is anxiety such a fearsome foe? Isn't it just another feeling, similar to joy, anger, or love? But what if some of our anxious feelings originate from *nowhere*? What if our misbeliefs and misconceptions about anxiety lead to anxiety itself?

In the Psalms, David implores God …

> "Guide me in your truth and teach me,
> for you are God my Savior,
> and my hope is in you all day long."
> Psalm 25:5

▶ **Myth:** "Because I have an anxiety disorder, I should always avoid whatever makes me feel anxious."

Truth: Avoiding what makes you anxious can actually make you feel even more anxiety. Instead of alleviating the angst, avoidance can actually reinforce anxiety. You will likely find that you can ultimately work through an anxious situation when you face it.

▶ **Myth:** "I'm afraid of passing out if I have a panic attack."

Truth: Fainting is unlikely because it's often caused by a sudden drop in blood pressure. During a panic attack, blood pressure doesn't fall, it rises slightly.

▶ **Myth:** "All medications for anxiety are addictive, so they should only be taken when absolutely necessary."

Truth: The use of certain medications, such as selective serotonin reuptake inhibitor (SSRI) antidepressants taken when a serotonin imbalance triggers anxiety, are not addictive. Benzodiazepines (which can relieve certain symptoms in social anxiety) might help for a short period of time (two weeks or less), but prolonged use can lead to higher tolerance, dependence, and severe adverse reactions to withdrawal. Symptoms related to performance anxiety respond well to beta-blockers, but are not considered effective for generalized anxiety disorder (GAD).[21] (Always consult with a physician or qualified, licensed practitioner about medical treatments.)

▶ **Myth:** "Medication is the only treatment available for anxiety."

Truth: Research shows that medication is helpful, but cognitive behavioral therapy (CBT) may be just as effective or produce even better results when used in conjunction with medication.

▶ **Myth:** "If I live a more healthy lifestyle (eating right, exercising, sleeping well, etc.), my anxiety will go away."

Truth: Maintaining a healthy lifestyle is certainly beneficial, but treating anxiety disorders usually requires more than just reducing stress. Facing fears, learning about symptoms, ending avoidance, and learning tolerance of some symptoms can also change how you think, feel, and behave.

▶ **Myth:** "My anxiety is not a problem because my family and friends understand and accept me as I am."

Truth: Acceptance and reassurance is a loving offer of support, but compassion can also be expressed by encouraging a loved one with anxiety to bravely address the challenge of seeking solutions.

▶ **Myth:** "Some people are just naturally anxious, neurotic, or worrywarts. Nothing really makes a difference."

Truth: While some people may have a predisposition to worry and exhibit anxious thoughts, regardless of temperament, beneficial therapy can reduce anxiety.

CAUSES

If you've ever seen an old tree or one that has been dug up, you know that roots can grow deep and are often intertwined. With some roots visible on the surface, others go down deep into the ground. Some are small, weak, and fragile while others are large, strong, and resilient (which explains why it's often difficult to pull a simple plant or weed out of the ground). And many times, roots overlap and interconnect so that it's hard to distinguish where one ends and another begins.

The causes of anxiety are much like the roots of a tree. Surface level causes (situational or environmental factors) exist, and so do deeply rooted, complex causes that relate to physical, mental, emotional, and spiritual well-being. These causes can overlap and interact in a variety of ways.

Although the causes may be complicated, the Lord wants us to continue to look to Him and trust Him in every struggle—including anxiety.

"Blessed is the man who trusts in the Lord,
whose trust is the Lord.
He is like a tree planted by water,
that sends out its roots by the stream,
and does not fear when heat comes,
for its leaves remain green,
and is not anxious in the year of drought,
for it does not cease to bear fruit."
Jeremiah 17:7–8 ESV

King David once pleaded with God, "*Search me, God, and know my heart; test me and know my anxious thoughts. See if there is any offensive way in me, and lead me in the way everlasting*" (Psalm 139:23–24). What a remarkable prayer! After reading a few psalms, you'll understand that David frequently struggled with anxious thoughts. But here, we see David *inviting God into his anxiety*.

As you uncover the various roots and causes of anxiety, invite God into the process. He cares about your heart, your thoughts, and your pain. He cares about *you*. He wants you to stay rooted in Him every step of the way.

> "And now, just as you accepted
> Christ Jesus as your Lord,
> you must continue to follow him.
> Let your roots grow down into him,
> and let your lives be built on him.
> Then your faith will grow strong
> in the truth you were taught,
> and you will overflow with thankfulness."
> Colossians 2:6–7 NLT

Common factors that play a role in causing or contributing to anxiety include:[22]

▶ **Threats**—Anxiety often occurs when a real or imagined threat appears. Threats can come from a variety of sources: new, unsafe, or unstable environments or social situations; being separated from loved ones and those who impart safety;

experiencing loss (of a job, loved one, home, beliefs, values, etc.). Threats can make people feel fearful, uncertain, helpless, and trapped—all of which can contribute to anxiety.

▶ **Conflicts**—Interpersonal conflicts or internal conflicts can lead to anxiety because they typically involve opposing ideas, interests, choices, forces, etc. This can create pressure, stress, fear, and uncertainty which can contribute to anxiety.

▶ **Stress**—Accumulated stress over time from difficult life events, relationship troubles, major transitions, losses, trauma, or other stressful situations can increase the risk of experiencing anxiety—especially if stressors remain unresolved for long periods of time.

▶ **Fear**—Closely related to anxiety, fear of certain objects, places, situations, activities, or people can gradually increase over time and become more and more persistent. This increase also elevates anxiety. Some fears are real, but oftentimes many are imagined or based on an irrational belief. Fears frequently develop from traumatic experiences or being conditioned (learning to associate the feeling of fear and anxiety with a particular object or situation).

▶ **Emotions**—How well a person handles and expresses emotions—particularly negative emotions like anger, frustration, or sadness—can contribute to anxiety. Denying, repressing, or not being allowed to express emotions, especially over a long period of time, often serves to increase anxiety.

▶ **Unmet Needs**—When basic, survival needs are not met, or even when deeper needs for purpose, meaning, significance, security, and identity are not satisfied, it can lead to feeling fearful, worried, insecure, uncertain, and anxious.

▶ **Biological Influences**—Substance abuse (drugs and alcohol), medical conditions, certain medications, excessive caffeine or nicotine, diet, lack of sleep, muscle tension, genetic factors, gender, and brain chemistry are all influential factors for anxiety. Hypochondriasis (constantly worrying about your health) can contribute to anxiety.[23]

▶ **Personality and Individual Differences**—Perfectionism, people-pleasing, and procrastination are common characteristics of those who struggle with anxiety.[24] Other individual differences related to personality, such as emotional sensitivity, can also contribute to anxiety.

▶ **Family and Upbringing**—Those whose parents struggled with anxiety are often more likely to struggle with it as well. Heredity may play a part, but witnessing and experiencing anxiety in other family members could be a learned response to becoming more anxious. Unhealthy coping mechanisms can contribute to anxiety. Those who grow up with critical, perfectionistic, abusive, neglectful, overprotective, or absent parents often feel a perpetual sense of unworthiness or insecurity, which can contribute to anxiety.

▶ **Coping Skills**—How well a person copes with stress and fear, whether approaching problems directly or avoiding them—including the use of medicine, drugs, and alcohol—can increase or decrease anxiety.

▶ **Self-Talk**—Constant negative ("I can't"), fearful ("What if"), and self-condemning ("I'm a failure") thoughts can contribute to anxiety as they anticipate bad outcomes and train a person to feel unable to handle a situation.

▶ **Beliefs**—Underlying beliefs about yourself, God, others, and the world at large can contribute to anxiety. For example, if you believe God is unloving and harsh, you will likely feel more fearful and worried. But if you believe God is gracious and compassionate, you will likely find more peace.

WHAT CAUSES the Physical Reactions of Anxiety?

The human body is marvelously made with its parts working in harmony with one another.

In the case of panic attacks, the brain perceives the body to be in danger and in need of protection. The brain methodically sends out a signal throughout the rest of the body to prepare for physical action, to be on the alert and ready to fight or take flight. That preparation includes all of the symptoms involved in a panic attack.

> "Distress and anguish fill him with terror;
> troubles overwhelm him,
> like a king poised to attack."
> Job 15:24

Much like a security system, by God's design, the body quickly responds to potential threats. Once activated, the body makes physiological preparations. When your body is in *emergency response mode* these physical symptoms can seem frightening, but the reasons for them are so the body can respond effectively and efficiently. However, in anxiety, your security system becomes extremely or overly sensitive and the body may not distinguish between actual danger and a perceived threat.

▶ **Why** the pounding heart—the rapid heartbeat?

Reason: The internal emergency response system switches on so the heart beats faster and harder pumping "fuel" (blood) to large muscle groups for rapid, powerful movement.

▶ **Why** the rapid breathing—feeling of not getting enough air?

Reason: Large muscle groups need oxygen as well as blood so breathing increases to force the oxygen to muscles.

▶ **Why** the perspiration—sweaty palms and skin?

Reason: Heat is created by muscles using up fuel so sweat is produced to regulate body temperature and also make it more difficult for an attacker to grasp and hold.

▶ **Why** the tingling or numbing sensations in the skin?

Reason: Blood tends to flow away from the skin to deep muscle tissue.

▶ **Why** the muscle tension or tightness?

Reason: Muscles tighten in preparation for "fight or flight" response.

▶ **Why** the dizziness, light-headedness, and poor concentration?

Reason: During extreme danger, blood may actually flow away from the brain.

▶ **Why** the nausea or knots in the stomach?

Reason: Digestion is suspended as blood is directed to large muscle groups rather than to the digestive system.

▶ **Why** the physical symptoms of danger when there is no danger?

Reason: Your brain has perceived danger or a threat and has triggered your internal emergency response system.

Truly, the psalmist was right when he said ...

> "I praise you because I am fearfully
> and wonderfully made;
> your works are wonderful,
> I know that full well."
> Psalm 139:14

Because anxiety has so many physical components, anyone suffering from it should get a thorough medical check-up, especially if the level of anxiety interferes with normal functioning. Be specific in describing any anxiety symptoms to your doctor. Ask the doctor to evaluate all your medications. Find out if any of the medications could contribute to anxiety or fear. Talk with a counselor or someone who specializes in anxiety disorders for treatment options.

> "Plans fail for lack of counsel,
> but with many advisers they succeed."
> Proverbs 15:22

▶ **Medical Conditions**—Anxiety is a symptom of certain medical conditions such as hypoglycemia, hyperthyroidism, congestive heart failure, chronic obstructive pulmonary disease (COPD), asthma, seizure disorders, and other conditions.[25] Talk with your doctor to determine if your anxiety may be due to a medical condition.

▶ **Substance/Medication-Induced**—The classification called *Substance/Medication-Induced Anxiety Disorder* is so named because of its causal relationship to fearful anxiety. Substances such as alcohol, caffeine, cannabis, drugs, inhalants, medications, stimulants, and toxins can cause anxiety, and the withdrawal from certain substances can also cause anxiety.[26]

▶ **Gender**—Anxiety disorders occur more frequently (about twice as often) in women than in men.[27]

They also occur earlier in women. This may be due to differences in brain chemistry, as "the brain system involved in the fight-or-flight response is activated more readily in women and stays activated longer than in men, partly as a result of the action of estrogen and progesterone [female hormones]."[28]

▶ **Diet**—Excessive caffeine can contribute to anxiety. Sugar levels can also play a factor (for example, anxiety is a symptom of hypoglycemia, low blood sugar). Certain substances can stress the body (salt and preservatives, for example). Eating habits, such as consuming too much or eating too fast, can also contribute to anxiety, as it often serves to stress the body.[29]

▶ **Sleep**—Anxiety can contribute to difficulty sleeping, which can then make dealing with the condition even more troublesome. A lack of sleep can also heighten stress hormones like adrenaline.[30]

▶ **Muscle Tension**—Muscle relaxation techniques are often used to treat anxiety because anxiety can cause physical tension all over the body. Calming the body often serves to calm the mind.[31]

▶ **Genetic Factors**—Some research suggests that anxiety disorders can run in families, indicating possible genetic factors that contribute to anxiety, but it could also be due to environmental factors in the home or behaviors learned from anxious parents.[32]

▶ **Biochemical Factors**—Some research suggests that chemical malfunctions or hormonal imbalances in the brain and/or body can cause anxiety. Having too much or too little of certain hormones can affect your mood and functioning. Biochemical causes may have further underlying causes, such as hereditary factors or stress. Talk with your doctor to address any concerns about hormonal or biochemical factors and possible treatments.[33]

WHAT Emotions Increase Anxiety?

Emotions can often make anxiety go from bad to worse. It's not clear whether certain emotions *cause* anxiety, but some emotions can make anxiety worse by increasing its intensity, extending its duration, or hindering the ability to cope. Another important factor is how emotions are handled. Anxiety can worsen when emotions are ignored or "stuffed," or if they are not expressed.

Remember, for every emotion we experience, God is never surprised. He knows what we are feeling and He wants us to come to Him with everything.

> "In my distress I prayed to the LORD,
> and the LORD answered me
> and set me free."
> Psalm 118:5 NLT

▶ **Fear**—Fear relates to anxiety as a primary emotion. Both fear and anxiety perceive a threat. The DSM-5 explains that "fear is the emotional response to real or perceived imminent threat, whereas anxiety is the anticipation of a future threat."[34] Whether a fear is real or imagined, it can trigger the fight or flight response and lead to anxiety.

"When I am afraid, I put my trust in you"
(Psalm 56:3).

▶ **Anger**—Similar to anxiety, anger can be a response to a threat—a threat to your livelihood, your loved ones, your beliefs, or your goals. Anger and anxiety seem to respond to a threat in a similar manner—they propel you to take action against a threat, either to guard or attack something. For example, if you're anxious about a test, you're more likely to be "on edge" and short with people or to become angry or lash out at others if they interrupt your studying. So anger can end up becoming one way to express or manage anxiety.

"'Don't sin by letting anger control you.' Don't let the sun go down while you are still angry"
(Ephesians 4:26 NLT).

▶ **Low Self-worth**—Maybe you lack confidence and think that people will reject you, so you avoid others or never reveal your true self. This dynamic can increase anxiety. A cycle can develop where you avoid people or situations to manage fear and anxiety, but then feelings of low self-worth continue and so does anxiety.

"He made us accepted in the Beloved"
(Ephesians 1:6 NKJV).

▶ **Depression**—Anxiety is often a feature of depression. The two also share similar characteristics such as irritability, sleeping problems, trouble concentrating, and avoidant behavior. The interaction between depression and anxiety can take numerous forms. For example, anxiety may cause you to avoid going out in public, and if that continues over time, it could contribute to depression. Then the depression may intensify anxiety when you have to go out.

"The LORD my God lightens my darkness. … He is a shield for all those who take refuge in him" (Psalm 18:28, 30 ESV).

▶ **Guilt**—There is *true guilt* (based in actual wrongdoing for not living according to God's standards) and *false guilt* (based in self-condemnation for not living up to your own standards or someone else's). False guilt (as well as misplaced guilt) arises when you blame yourself even though you've committed no wrong—or it occurs even after you have already confessed and turned from your sin. The anxiety associated with guilt may be due in part to the fear of judgment or of facing the consequences of wrongful actions. God wants you to relinquish any false guilt you feel and turn to Him when you experience true guilt so He can forgive you and remove your guilt.

"I confessed all my sins to you and stopped trying to hide my guilt. I said to myself, 'I will confess my rebellion to the LORD.' And you forgave me! All my guilt is gone" (Psalm 32:5 NLT).

▶ **Grief**—When we suffer loss, especially of a loved one, we normally experience grief. If you're prone to anxiety, grief can intensify this condition. You may start to worry and fear the loss of someone else or that you might die soon. These fears and worries may lead to you becoming more cautious and closed off from personal relationships.

"I, yes I, am the one who comforts you" (Isaiah 51:12 NLT).

WHAT ARE the Spiritual Causes of Anxiety?

If you've ever ridden on public transportation such as a bus, a train, or especially a plane, you know the anxiety that can accompany such a ride. You're not in control of the driver's or pilot's seat, where you're going, who's going with you, or when you will get there. The whole experience can cause anxiety because you simply don't know what's going to happen. Yet, every day, millions of people get on buses, trains, and planes. They sit down and trust that the driver or pilot will take them where they need to go.

When we experience anxiety, we often don't trust that God is in control. We believe that we need to take control of the wheel—or simply avoid traveling altogether. What our anxiety actually reveals is distrust in God's goodness, sovereignty, and presence in our lives. How we think about and relate to God can impact our anxiety and our response to anxiety. Just as there are physical, mental, and emotional causes of anxiety, so too there are spiritual causes.

In the midst of our fears and worries, God calls us to seek Him and trust Him.

"Those who know your name trust in you,
for you, LORD, have never forsaken
those who seek you."
Psalm 9:10

Distorted View of God

If you believe God is harsh and "out to get you" or that He is not good, not in control, or simply doesn't care about you, then you will likely have fear and anxiety—that it's up to you to hold everything together in your life. But if you believe God is loving and is *for you*—that He is good, in control, and does care about you—then you're more likely to experience peace in your life. You won't feel the need to control everything or believe that your well-being is completely up to you. Thankfully, God *is* good, He *is* in control, and He *does* care about you—even empathizes with you. When you're anxious, He welcomes you to come to Him to find help and hope.

The Bible says, *"For we do not have a high priest who is unable to empathize with our weaknesses, but we have one who has been tempted in every way, just as we are—yet he did not sin. Let us then approach God's throne of grace with confidence, so that we may receive mercy and find grace to help us in our time of need"* (Hebrews 4:15–16).

Idolatry

Whenever we make something "ultimate" in our lives or make anything—either good or bad—more important than God, we practice idolatry. No person, experience, or thing can meet our deepest longings except God. When we make someone or something into an idol, we can become fearful or anxious that we might lose them or fear being rejected. But when God is at the center of our lives, we never have to worry about Him leaving or rejecting us because He accepts us on the basis of His mercy and grace (not because of what we do) and He promises to never leave us.

The Lord says, *"I have chosen you and have not rejected you. So do not fear, for I am with you; do not be dismayed, for I am your God. I will strengthen you and help you; I will uphold you with my righteous right hand"* (Isaiah 41:9–10).

Sin

Sin can also lead to anxiety because of the guilt associated with sin. When King David sinned, he wrote about his crushing guilt: *"My guilt has overwhelmed me like a burden too heavy to bear"* (Psalm 38:4). Thankfully, God's grace and forgiveness can break through sin, guilt, fear, and anxiety. We don't have to fear or worry that God will withhold forgiveness when we confess our sin.

The Bible says, *"O Lord, you are so good, so ready to forgive, so full of unfailing love for all who ask for your help"* (Psalm 86:5 NLT).

Trials

Any conflict or difficulty has the potential to create anxiety. When a trial threatens, you might worry about the outcome, feel under-equipped to handle the problem, or just be generally overwhelmed. The Bible repeatedly shows that God allows trials to test our faith and refine our character. Rather than presenting trials as occasions for anxiety, they are presented as opportunities.

"Consider it pure joy, my brothers and sisters, whenever you face trials of many kinds, because you know that the testing of your faith produces perseverance. Let perseverance finish its work so that you may be mature and complete, not lacking anything" (James 1:2–4).

Response to Suffering

God cares about the suffering and anxiety we face. In fact, He tells us directly, *"Cast all your anxiety on him because he cares for you"* (1 Peter 5:7). Prayer, or any spiritual discipline, is not a catch-all fix to suffering and anxiety, but we often forfeit God's peace in the midst of suffering and anxiety because we don't go to Him. We carry unnecessary burdens, sacrifice peace, and increase our worries when we don't trust God. But God, out of the infinite riches of His grace, continues to call us to pour out our hearts to Him and trust Him for rest and refuge.

The Bible says, *"Yes, my soul, find rest in God; my hope comes from him. … Trust in him at all times, you people; pour out your hearts to him, for God is our refuge"* (Psalm 62:5, 8).

Unbelief

Jesus connected anxiety and unbelief when He said, *"Do not be anxious about your life, what you will eat or what you will drink, nor about your body, what you will put on. … O you of little faith"* (Matthew 6:25, 30 ESV). In short, Jesus says, *"Do not be anxious … O you of little faith."* Anxiety can sometimes reveal a lack of faith in God to meet our needs and take care of us. Jesus reminds us that God takes care of even birds and flowers, so He will certainly not overlook our needs but will take care of us. When we're anxious, Jesus calls us to faith—to put our focus on God and seek Him above all else.

Jesus says, *"Seek first the kingdom of God and his righteousness, and all these things will be added to you. Therefore do not be anxious about tomorrow, for tomorrow will be anxious for itself. Sufficient for the day is its own trouble"* (Matthew 6:33–34 ESV).

Satanic Influences

Not all anxiety is traceable to the devil and demonic forces, but the Bible is clear about their work in the world and our lives. They stand in opposition to who God is and what He does. Jesus said that the devil is a *"murderer from the beginning, not holding to the truth, for there is no truth in him. When he lies, he speaks his native language, for he is a liar and the father of lies"* (John 8:44). Satan is also called the *"accuser of our brothers and sisters, who accuses them before our God day and night"* (Revelation 12:10). While God speaks truth and invites you to live in His love, grace, and peace, the devil speaks lies, accuses, and seeks to consume you with constant doubt, guilt, and fear. Satan wants anxiety to draw you away from God, but God wants you to stand firm on His truth and draw nearer to Him.

The Bible says, *"Be strong in the Lord and in his mighty power. Put on all of God's armor so that you will be able to stand firm against all strategies of the devil"* (Ephesians 6:10–11 NLT).

Saint Francis de Sales wrote, "Anxiety is a temptation in itself and also the source from and by which other temptations come."[35] In other words, when we experience anxiety, we are tempted with other things. Suppose you're anxious about not passing an exam; you may then be tempted to cheat. If you're anxious about how you will pay your bills, you may be tempted to gamble. If you're anxious about a loved one, you may be tempted to abuse alcohol or drugs. As you try to alleviate the discomfort of anxiety, you can be tempted to do so in unhealthy ways. When you feel anxious, look to God and remind yourself that He is faithful to help.

The Bible says, *"The temptations in your life are no different from what others experience. And God is faithful. He will not allow the temptation to be more than you can stand. When you are tempted, he will show you a way out so that you can endure"* (1 Corinthians 10:13 NLT).

WHAT IS the Spiritual Root Cause of Anxiety?

God calls us to stand in *His strength* when we are filled with anxiety. Rather than being paralyzed and controlled by fear and anxiety, we can trust in and rely on God.

> "It is God who arms me with strength
> and keeps my way secure."
> Psalm 18:32

Three Inner Needs

We all have three inner needs: the needs for love, significance, and security.[36]

▶ **Love**—to know that someone is unconditionally committed to our best interest

"My command is this: Love each other as I have loved you" (John 15:12).

▶ **Significance**—to know that our lives have meaning and purpose

"I cry out to God Most High, to God, who fulfills his purpose for me" (Psalm 57:2 ESV).

▶ **Security**—to feel accepted and a sense of belonging

"Whoever fears the LORD has a secure fortress, and for their children it will be a refuge" (Proverbs 14:26).

The Ultimate Need-Meeter

What do our inner needs reveal about us and our relationship with God?

God did not create any person or position or any amount of power or possessions to meet our deepest needs. People fail us and self-effort also fails to meet our deepest needs. If a person or thing could meet all our needs, we wouldn't need God! Our inner needs draw us into a deeper dependence on Christ and remind us that only God can satisfy the longings of our hearts. The Lord brings people and circumstances into our lives as an extension of His care, but ultimately only He can satisfy all the needs of our hearts.

The Bible says …

> "The LORD will guide you always;
> he will satisfy your needs in a sun-scorched
> land and will strengthen your frame.
> You will be like a well-watered garden,
> like a spring whose waters never fail."
> Isaiah 58:11

All along, the Lord planned to meet our deepest needs for …

▶ **Love**—*"I [the Lord] have loved you with an everlasting love; I have drawn you with unfailing kindness"* (Jeremiah 31:3).

▶ **Significance**—*"'For I know the plans I have for you,' declares the LORD, 'plans to prosper you and not to harm you, plans to give you hope and a future'"* (Jeremiah 29:11).

▶ **Security**—*"The LORD himself goes before you and will be with you; he will never leave you nor forsake you. Do not be afraid; do not be discouraged"* (Deuteronomy 31:8).

Our needs for love, significance, and security can be legitimately met in Christ Jesus! Philippians 4:19 makes it plain …

> "My God will meet all your needs
> according to the riches of his glory
> in Christ Jesus."

▶ **WRONG BELIEF**

"God is disappointed with me for having anxiety. He probably doesn't care about me or my situation anyway. Nothing can be done about my anxiety. I have no control over my anxiety, so my only option is to avoid all anxiety-producing situations."

▶ **Right Belief**

"God loves me and cares about every aspect of my life. I can face my anxiety in the strength of the Lord. With God's help, I can focus my thoughts on His truth and character. I will seek His wisdom to guide and direct me to whatever help I need. I will look to God for strength and peace to calm my fearful heart, and I will trust Him with my life and every anxiety-producing situation."

"The Lord is my strength and my shield;
my heart trusts in him, and he helps me."
Psalm 28:7

HOW CAN You Find God's Peace Amidst Anxiety?

Is anxiety weighing you down? Is your heart overwhelmed with fear and worry? Realize, the Bible says, *"Anxiety weighs down the heart, but a kind word cheers it up"* (Proverbs 12:25). The good news is that God has a kind word for you—a good word, a *life-giving* word to lift you out of the pit of anxiety. He wants you to know the *"word of truth, the gospel of your salvation"* (Ephesians 1:13 esv). The Lord does not want your heart weighed down with anxiety. Instead, He wants you to experience His peace, for *"a heart at peace gives life to the body"* (Proverbs 14:30). That peace comes through a personal relationship with Christ.

Jesus says to you …

"Peace I leave with you; my peace I give you.
I do not give to you as the world gives.
Do not let your hearts be troubled
and do not be afraid."
John 14:27

Four Points of God's Plan

Whether you're trying to make sense of your past, trying to overcome something in the present, or trying to make changes for a better future, the Lord cares about you. He loves you. No matter what challenges you or your loved ones are facing, no matter the pain or difficult feelings you may be experiencing, no matter what you've done or what's been done to you, there is hope. And that hope is found in Jesus Christ.

God has a plan for your life, and it begins with a personal relationship with Jesus. The most important decision you can ever make is whether you will receive His invitation. If you have never made that decision, these four simple truths can help you start your journey together with Him.

1. God's Purpose for You Is *Salvation.*

What was God's motivation in sending Jesus Christ to earth?

To express His love for you by saving you!

The Bible says, *"God so loved the world that he gave his one and only Son, that whoever believes in him shall not perish but have eternal life. For God did not send his Son into the world to condemn the world, but to save the world through him"* (John 3:16–17).

To forgive your sins, to empower you to have victory over sin, and to enable you to live a fulfilled life!

Jesus said, *"I have come that they may have life, and have it to the full"* (John 10:10).

2. The Problem Is *Sin.*

Sin is living independently of God's standard—knowing what is wrong and doing it anyway—also knowing what is right and choosing not to do it.

The apostle Paul said, *"I know that nothing good lives in me, that is, in my sinful nature. I want to do what is right, but I can't. I want to do what is good, but I don't. I don't want to do what is wrong, but I do it anyway"* (Romans 7:18–19 NLT).

Spiritual death, eternal separation from God.

The Bible says, *"Your iniquities [sins] have separated you from your God"* (Isaiah 59:2).

Scripture also says, *"The wages of sin is death, but the gift of God is eternal life in Christ Jesus our Lord"* (Romans 6:23).

3. God's Provision for You Is *the Savior.*

Yes! Jesus died on the cross to personally pay the penalty for your sins.

The Bible says, *"God demonstrates his own love for us in this: While we were still sinners, Christ died for us"* (Romans 5:8).

What is the solution to being separated from God?

Belief in (entrusting your life to) Jesus Christ as the only way to God the Father.

Jesus said, *"I am the way and the truth and the life. No one comes to the Father except through me"* (John 14:6).

The Bible says, *"Believe in the Lord Jesus, and you will be saved"* (Acts 16:31).

4. Your Part Is *Surrender.*

Give Christ control of your life, entrusting yourself to Him.

Jesus said, *"Whoever wants to be my disciple must deny themselves and take up their cross and follow me. For whoever wants to save their life will lose it, but whoever loses their life for me will find it. What good will it be for someone to gain the whole world, yet forfeit their soul?"* (Matthew 16:24–26).

Place your faith in (rely on) Jesus Christ as your personal Lord and Savior and reject your "good works" as a means of earning God's approval.

The Bible says, *"It is by grace you have been saved, through faith—and this is not from yourselves, it is the gift of God—not by works, so that no one can boast"* (Ephesians 2:8–9).

Has there been a time in your life when you know you've humbled your heart and received Jesus Christ as your personal Lord and Savior—giving Him control of your life? You can tell God that you want to surrender your life to Christ in a simple, heartfelt prayer, like the following prayer.

PRAYER OF SALVATION

"God, I want a real relationship with you.
I admit that many times
I've chosen to go my own way
instead of your way.
Please forgive me for my sins.
Jesus, thank you for dying on the cross
to pay the penalty for my sins.
Come into my life to be my Lord
and my Savior.
Change me from the inside out
and make me the person
you created me to be.
In your holy name I pray. Amen."

WHAT CAN YOU NOW EXPECT?

When you surrender your life to Christ, you receive the Holy Spirit who empowers you to live a life pleasing to God. The Bible says, *"His divine power has given us everything we need for a godly life"* (2 Peter 1:3).

Jesus assures those who believe with these words ...

"Truly I tell you, whoever hears my word
and believes him who sent me
has eternal life and will not be judged
but has crossed over from death to life."
John 5:24

STEPS TO SOLUTION

Scripture instructs us to cast all of our cares on the Lord, to commit and entrust our desires and concerns entirely to Him. But how do we do that?

A sheep that falls over and ends up on its back has a difficult time getting on its feet again. Its legs will flail and it may cry and bleat. Such a sheep is rendered helpless. This position is referred to as "cast down."

Sheep have an uncanny ability to lay there and do nothing. Without resources to remedy the situation, a sheep gives up and waits to die. When we are anxious, we are like cast sheep with no inner resources to affect our situation. But we do have an incredible resource available to us: Jesus *wants* us to depend on Him. Rather than remaining "cast," we can trust Him and cast all our anxieties on Him.

KEY VERSE TO MEMORIZE

"Cast all your anxiety on him because he cares for you."
1 Peter 5:7

Key Passage to Read

Consider this remarkable truth: God, the creator of all things, cares uniquely about *you*. David, once a shepherd himself, was stunned by this truth, saying,

"When I consider your heavens, the work of your fingers, the moon and the stars, which you have set in place, what is mankind that you are mindful of them, human beings that you care for them?" (Psalm 8:3–4).

God not only cares about you and the specifics of your life, but He has also given precise instructions to combat anxiety. He speaks directly to this issue, and He speaks directly to you.

Philippians 4:4–9

4 Rejoice in the Lord always.
I will say it again: Rejoice!
5 Let your gentleness be evident to all.
The Lord is near.
6 Do not be anxious about anything,
but in every situation,
by prayer and petition, with thanksgiving,
present your requests to God.
7 And the peace of God, which transcends
all understanding, will guard your hearts
and your minds in Christ Jesus.
8 Finally, brothers and sisters, whatever is true,
whatever is noble, whatever is right,
whatever is pure, whatever is lovely,
whatever is admirable—
if anything is excellent or praiseworthy—
think about such things.
9 Whatever you have learned or received
or heard from me, or seen in me—
put it into practice. And the God of
peace will be with you.

▶ **Find** your joy in the unchanging God, not in changing circumstances. (v. 4)

▶ **Be** gentle and gracious (with yourself and others) instead of harsh and condemning. (v. 5)

▶ **Remember** that the Lord is near you, and He will return to renew all things. (v. 5)

▶ **Talk** with God about anything and everything that causes you anxiety. (v. 6)

▶ **Tell** God about the situation and how you're feeling, and ask Him to help. (v. 6)

▶ **Thank** God for who He is and what He has done for you. (v. 6)

▶ **Receive** God's peace, which is given to you through Jesus Christ. (v. 7)

▶ **Fix** your thoughts on what is true and positive instead of what is false and negative. (v. 8)

▶ **Recall** the wisdom you have learned from others and practice it regularly. (v. 9)

▶ **Remember,** above all, that God is the God of peace and He is with you. (v. 9)

God's Sovereignty

QUESTION: "How can knowing that God is sovereign help me overcome fear and anxiety?"

ANSWER: The word *sovereign* means that God has ultimate authority over everything. As the creator and sustainer of everything, He has power and control over all things. His sovereignty also means that He is absolutely free to do whatever He wants within the context of His character to fulfill His will. His ways will always be perfectly holy, just, loving, and wise.

The Bible shows God's sovereign activity in a variety of ways:

▶ **He is in control of every outcome in life.**

"We may throw the dice, but the Lord determines how they fall" (Proverbs 16:33 NLT).

▶ **He determines exactly how long each of us will live**.

"You have decided the length of our lives. You know how many months we will live, and we are not given a minute longer" (Job 14:5 NLT).

▶ **He can even use sin and evil to accomplish His good purposes**.

"You intended to harm me, but God intended it for good" (Genesis 50:20).

When Jesus talked about worry and anxiety, He also talked about God's sovereignty:

▶ He providentially feeds the birds of the air and clothes the flowers of the field (Matthew 6:25–29).

▶ He further hinted at God's sovereignty in saying, *"Your heavenly Father already knows all your needs"* (Matthew 6:32 NLT).

▶ He also knows your every thought (Psalm 139:2), every word (Psalm 139:4), every action (Psalm 139:2–3), and every intention of your heart (1 Chronicles 28:9).

Realize, nothing that happens in your life occurs outside of God's sovereign knowledge, ultimate authority, and providential care. When you're filled with anxiety, when it feels like your life is coming apart at the seams, the truth of God's sovereignty can give you hope, peace, security, and confidence. Rest in the knowledge that God is in control—*so you don't have to be.* Remember that He can use any circumstance for good (Romans 8:28), and allow that truth to calm your greatest fears and wash away your worries. Let His sovereignty drive you to Him—to cling to Him and rest in Him and praise Him.

"Blessed are you, O LORD, the God of
Israel our father, forever and ever.
Yours, O LORD, is the greatness
and the power
and the glory and the victory
and the majesty,
for all that is in the heavens
and in the earth is yours.
Yours is the kingdom, O LORD, and you
are exalted as head above all.
Both riches and honor come from you,
and you rule over all.
In your hand are power and might,
and in your hand it is to make great
and to give strength to all.
And now we thank you, our God,
and praise your glorious name."
1 Chronicles 29:10–13 ESV

Anxiety can divide our attention and sap our energy. We often assume anxiety is a negative force—something to tear down and defeat. One therapist and author (who also struggles with anxiety) posed this question to a client and himself: "What if God put anxiety in your life for a purpose? … What if God is saying, 'Pay attention to me. Don't get stuck and buried in your fears.' What if anxiety is God's catalyst to help you grow?"[37]

REACHING THE TARGET: TRANSFORMATION!

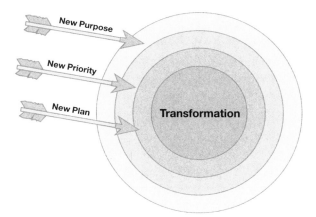

THE FREEDOM FORMULA

	A New Purpose
+	A New Priority
+	A New Plan

A Transformed Life

Target 1—A New Purpose: God's purpose for me is to be conformed to the character of Christ.

> *"Those God foreknew he also predestined to be conformed to the image of his Son"* (Romans 8:29).

- "I'll do whatever it takes to be conformed to the character of Christ."

Target 2—A New Priority: God's priority for me is to change my thinking.

> *"Do not conform to the pattern of this world, but be transformed by the renewing of your mind"* (Romans 12:2).

- "I'll do whatever it takes to line up my thinking with God's thinking."

Target 3—A New Plan: God's plan for me is to rely on Christ's strength, not my strength, to be all He created me to be.

> *"I can do all things through Christ who strengthens me"* (Philippians 4:13 NKJV).

- "I'll do whatever it takes to fulfill His plan in His strength."

My Personalized Plan

For those who wrestle with anxiety, the future can feel bleak—void of hope and joy but full of fear and misfortune. But God always offers hope for the future and help for today. He comes alongside you and says, *"Do not fear, for I am with you"* (Isaiah 41:10). To the fearful heart, the Bible says, *"With his love, he will calm all your fears"* (Zephaniah 3:17 NLT).

With God's help, you can move forward today and have hope for tomorrow.

> "There is surely a future hope for you,
> and your hope will not be cut off."
> Proverbs 23:18

As I seek God's help with my anxiety, I will …

▶ **Remember God's character.**

- I will seek to know God's character by reading His Word and praying for Him to continually reveal Himself to me.

- I will believe that God is good, that He is with me, and that He will help me—and trust that He is in control and has my best interests at heart.

"The Lord is gracious and compassionate, slow to anger and rich in love. The Lord is good to all; he has compassion on all he has made. … The Lord is trustworthy in all he promises and faithful in all he does" (Psalm 145:8–9, 13).

▶ **Address physical issues.**

- I will talk with a doctor about the symptoms I am experiencing and seek treatment.

- I will seek to maintain a healthy lifestyle by eating well, exercising regularly, getting plenty of rest, staying hydrated, avoiding harmful substances, and learning relaxation techniques to manage stress and anxiety.

"I discipline my body and keep it under control" (1 Corinthians 9:27 ESV).

▶ **Talk with others.**

- I will seek the help of a professional counselor, supportive group of people in my church or community, and/or talk with trusted friends and family members.

- I will be honest about how I'm feeling and what I'm experiencing.

"Where there is no guidance the people fall, but in abundance of counselors there is victory" (Proverbs 11:14 NASB).

▶ **Reorient my thoughts.**

- I will keep a journal and write down my honest thoughts.

- I will seek to align my thoughts with God's Word, identifying thoughts that are based on lies and replacing them with God's truth.

"Whatever is true, whatever is noble, whatever is right, whatever is pure, whatever is lovely, whatever is admirable—if anything is excellent or praiseworthy— think about such things" (Philippians 4:8).

▶ **Be in community.**

- I will regularly meet with friends and family members to talk, share a meal, or go out together.

- I will look into joining a local church, small group, Bible study, or community support group.

"Two people are better off than one, for they can help each other succeed. If one person falls, the other can reach out and help" (Ecclesiastes 4:9–10 NLT).

▶ **Stay active spiritually.**

- I will maintain an active spiritual life by praying, reading God's Word, and meeting with other believers to help me grow.

- I will constantly seek to grow in my relationship with Christ, who loves me and gives me grace each day.

"Grow in the grace and knowledge of our Lord and Savior Jesus Christ" (2 Peter 3:18).

▶ **Hang on to hope.**

- I will remember that true, lasting hope is found not in my circumstances but in God and His Word.

- I will mediate on God's promises in the Bible, remembering that I can always have hope.

"Everything that was written in the past was written to teach us, so that through the endurance taught in the Scriptures and the encouragement they provide we might have hope" (Romans 15:4).

HOW TO Calm Your Body—*Physically*

When the winds of fearful circumstances blow into your life and the waves of anxiety crash into your mind, it can feel like you're drowning in chaotic waters. You can barely stay above the surface and catch your breath. But God has provided a way to find peace in the storm. He designed our bodies in such a way that we can calm ourselves down physically through a variety of techniques. Practicing these exercises can help you prepare for, and manage, the physical effects of anxiety.

> "When you go through deep waters,
> I will be with you.
> When you go through rivers of
> difficulty, you will not drown."
> Isaiah 43:2 NLT

▶ Breathing Techniques[38]

Deep abdominal breathing is a natural sedative that can be used to calm your body when you're experiencing anxiety. Here's what to do:

- Sit comfortably in a chair or lie down on your back with your hands resting on your chest.

- Slowly breathe in through your nose to the count of five.

- Hold your breath for three to five seconds.

- Slowly blow the air out through your mouth to the count of five.

- Repeat this deep abdominal breathing for three to five minutes several times a day until you experience its calming effects and become comfortable doing it.

▶ Muscle Relaxation[39]

Anxiety often leads to muscle tension, and feeling tense often leads to anxiety. By relaxing the muscles in your body, you can break the cycle and calm yourself. Do this one muscle group at a time throughout your whole body, for ten to fifteen minutes a day. Pair it with a deep breathing exercise.

Go through the following exercises, holding each muscle group for five to ten seconds, then relaxing and waiting fifteen to twenty seconds before moving on to the next muscle group.

- *Face:* Tighten your facial muscles ... hold ... relax, wait and breathe.

- *Neck and Shoulders:* Shrug your shoulders up, tensing your neck, chest and upper back ... hold ... relax, wait and breathe.

- *Arms:* Make a fist with one of your hands and flex your biceps ... hold ... relax, wait and breathe. Repeat using the other hand ... hold ... relax, wait and breathe.

- *Core:* Arch your back, tensing your stomach and lower back ... hold ... relax, wait and breathe.

- *Bottom:* Tighten your buttocks and pull in your abdomen ... hold ... relax, wait and breathe.

- *Thighs:* Tense the thighs in both legs ... hold ... relax, wait and breathe.

- *Calves:* Tense the calves in both legs ... hold ... relax, wait and breathe.

- *Feet:* Stretch out one of your legs and point your foot and toes down ... hold ... relax, wait and breathe. Stretch out the same leg and forcefully point your foot and toes up ... hold ... relax, wait and breathe. Repeat both exercises using the other leg ... hold ... relax, wait and breathe.

▶ **Physical Exercise**

- Stay physically active and exercise on a regular basis (following a doctor's recommendations) to build stamina and keep your body reasonably ready "to fight or take flight."

- Briskly walk or jog a minimum of ten minutes every day.

- Play handball, racquetball, basketball, tennis, ping-pong, soccer, or some other sport.

- Join a fitness center, ride a bicycle, swim or do water aerobics.

- Exert physical energy when you anticipate a panic attack.

▶ **Nutrition**[40]

What you eat can stress your body and increase anxiety or have a calming effect and reduce anxiety.

- Limit caffeine and nicotine, which can make you jittery and increase anxiety.

- Limit simple sugars, sweets, alcohol, and fried or processed foods.

- Avoid foods you are allergic to that stress your body.

- Drink plenty of water each day (six to eight glasses a day).

- Eat plenty of fresh vegetables.

- Keep your blood sugar stable (hypoglycemia, low blood sugar, can increase anxiety).

Medication

QUESTION: "What role, if any, does medication play in managing anxiety?"

ANSWER: Some people may be able to manage their anxiety and overcome it without medication, others might need medication temporarily to relieve severe symptoms, and still others might rely on certain medicines long term to make up for a chemical imbalance. Certainly, the decision of whether or not to use medication—and for how long—is best made with the recommendation of a qualified physician who closely monitors and manages appropriate care.

▶ Managing anxiety can feel like you're on a boat in the center of a storm in the middle of the ocean. Medication may help calm the storm, but *you still need to get to land*. While medication can help, there are still things you can do to help further manage anxiety such as seeking counseling, adjusting your automatic thoughts and beliefs, addressing emotional and spiritual needs, etc.

▶ Christians need not suffer for fear of being labeled "unspiritual" for seeking medical help when medication can help treat a biochemical imbalance. People often think if you have faith and pray more, the Lord will heal you. One anxiety sufferer explains it this way, "The Lord has led me to a good psychiatrist and good medicine. God is in the business of healing."[41]

▶ If you're considering using medication, do some research and talk with your doctor. Be sure to ask how long you will need to take medication and the potential short-term and long-term side effects (as well as potential interactions) of each drug your doctor might prescribe, as well as any recommended supplements. Also, talk with others who have used medication to help manage anxiety and get their feedback.

▶ The use of medication *is* biblical (see Ezekiel 47:12). However, medicine should *never* be used to avoid dealing with issues, to numb pain, or as an escape or "quick fix." Rather, it can be a tool to help those who suffer from severe anxiety. Additionally, medication is most often a complement to other avenues of treatment.

Striking the right balance of treatment options is unique for each individual and should be explored in conjunction with ongoing counseling and medical supervision. Medicine can be a gracious gift from God to help ease our discomfort and improve our health, but it is never to be our sole source for healing—that's God's place.

"Every good and perfect gift is from above, coming down from the Father of the heavenly lights." James 1:17

When you're anxious, you might feel like your thoughts and emotions are running wild. "Automatic" thoughts occur when we're anxious, and those thoughts are typically negative, untrue, and full of fear and worry (also known as Automatic Negative Thoughts or ANTs).

These thoughts need to be met with truth. It is imperative to focus your thoughts and redirect them on what is true and positive.

> "Fix your thoughts on what is true,
> and honorable, and right,
> and pure, and lovely, and admirable.
> Think about things that are excellent
> and worthy of praise."
> **Philippians 4:8** NLT

When you're anxious, think through the characteristics listed in Philippians 4:8.[42]

▶ **What is true?**

Ask yourself: What is true and accurate about my situation? What does God say I should do (or not do)? What promises of God or attribute of God can speak to my situation?

▶ **What is honorable?**

Ask yourself: What is the respectful thing to do in my situation? Is there someone I trust and respect who I can talk to about my anxiety? What can I do that will honor the Lord?

▶ What is right?

Ask yourself: What does God say is the right thing to do in my circumstance? What will happen if I do what is right? What will happen if I do what is wrong? Who can help me do what's right?

▶ What is pure?

Ask yourself: Is my anxiety leading me to God—to His presence, His Word, and His people? In what ways is my anxiety leading me away from God— tempting me to doubt God, control others, or sin?

▶ What is lovely?

Ask yourself: In what ways has the Lord shown His love to me? What do I love about God? How can I show love to God, to others, and to myself?

▶ What is admirable?

Ask yourself: Who can I speak well of or compliment? What aspects of my situation are good or commendable? Who has helped me (or is currently helping me) and deserves to be thanked?

▶ What is excellent?

Ask yourself: Are there any immoral thoughts or actions I need to confess and change? What morals, virtues, or godly characteristics do I need to work on, with God's help?

▶ What is praiseworthy?

Ask yourself: What am I thankful for in my situation? What things can I praise God for (relationships, spiritual and material blessings, knowledge, health, etc.)?

When seeking to control your anxious thoughts, remember that Jesus is the greatest thought you can have. That is why God says to *"fix your thoughts on Jesus"* (Hebrews 3:1). He is the most true, honorable, right, pure, lovely, admirable, excellent, and praiseworthy person in the world. And the great news is that Jesus is for you, with you, and in you. When anxiety weighs you down, He can lift you up and raise your thoughts to Him and the glorious future He has for you.

> "Set your minds on things above,
> not on earthly things.
> For you died, and your life
> is now hidden with Christ in God.
> When Christ, who is your life, appears,
> then you also will appear with him in glory."
> Colossians 3:2–4

HOW TO Corral Your Feelings— *Emotionally*[43]

With 40,000 neurons in the heart—as many as in important areas of the brain—the heart signals important information to the brain, especially the amygdala, which processes information with emotional significance. So, by God's design, the brain works in conjunction with the heart, giving each person intellectual cognition (through the brain) and intuitive perception (through the heart).

When anxiety intrudes, God offers us His peace to quiet our minds and soothe our hearts.

▶ **Tune in to your body.**

Feelings are usually simple or complex. Basic emotions are typically simple: anger, fear, sadness, love, and joy. Complex emotions may include an assorted mix of simple emotions, but are also more unique in how long they last and what triggers them. For example, you may feel love, anger, and guilt all at once if you are arguing with someone close to you.

- Physically relax (progressive muscle relaxation, meditation, or another relaxation technique for five to ten minutes when your body is tense and your mind is racing).

- Assess what you're feeling in the moment (main focus of concern).

- Concentrate where in your body you feel emotional sensations like anger, fear, or sadness (such as heart, stomach). Observe what feelings or moods surface by waiting for them. Revisit the previous steps beginning with relaxation if thoughts continue to race.

▶ **Express your feelings.**

Feelings are neither right nor wrong. They simply are. Thoughts, judgments, and perceptions that lead to feelings may be right or wrong, true or false. Thus, feelings are an indicator of your own conclusions, but not of someone else's motivations or actions.

- Ask the Lord to reveal your feelings to you.

- Express your feelings by sharing them with someone or writing your feelings in a journal.

- Release your feelings physically (by exercising or crying into a pillow).

▶ **Examine the need underlying your emotions.**

Feelings can be suppressed, but they tend to surface in one way or another, like bubbles that "rise to the surface or [turbulent] waves that you must ride out."[44] You could be mad at your spouse, and take that anger with you to work. You might hold your feelings in or distract yourself to avoid them. Burying feelings can result in a later unplanned eruption or an unseen internal implosion. You can also experience numbness or emotional emptiness if you remain out of touch with your feelings.

- If you're anxious because you're afraid of what others think, a need for acceptance might be causing your fear.

- If you're anxious when someone breaks a promise, a need for respect and appreciation could trigger your anger.

- If you're anxious when your life seems dull or routine, a need for meaning and purpose might be driving your depression.

When we stop and examine our circumstances, thoughts, emotions, and actions, they can reveal the core beliefs we have about ourselves, God, and life in general. These beliefs can all too often be based on lies that need to be challenged and confronted with God's truth.

What we say we believe doesn't always line up with what we practice or how we respond to stressful situations. We need to bring our thoughts, actions, emotions, and beliefs into alignment.

To break free from the deeply held lies we believe, we need to know the truth. Jesus said ...

> "You will know the truth,
> and the truth will set you free."
> John 8:32

When You Encounter Anxiety-Producing Situations:[45]

▶ **Identify the triggering event.**

- Where were you?

- Who were you with? Or were you alone?

- What exactly happened?

▶ **Examine your unhealthy responses.**

- What did you think? What was your automatic negative thought?

- What did you feel?

- What did you say?

- What did you do?

▶ **Evaluate your thoughts and beliefs.**[46]

- What does your response reveal about your core beliefs about you? About God?

- What evidence is there for these core beliefs? And does the evidence suggest that your belief is true or not true?

- Is there another way to understand what happened?

- What factors haven't you considered?

- What effect does this belief have on you?

▶ **Confront your beliefs with God's truth.**

- What passage of Scripture speaks to your belief, either to support or challenge it?

- Memorize and mediate on that passage or truth regularly. Write it down and read it often.

▶ **Plan for a healthy response in the future.**

- What thoughts do you need to watch for and challenge the next time this situation happens?

- What passage from God's Word do you need to remember?

- What do you need to pray for when you encounter this situation?

- What actions can you take that will be more helpful and healthy next time?

Mary sits peacefully at the feet of Jesus, listening to Him teach. Martha, busy with and distracted by "much serving" starts to get agitated. Martha tells Jesus that He needs to tell Mary to help her out. Jesus' reply is poignant: *"Martha, Martha, you are anxious and troubled about many things"* (Luke 10:41 ESV). Now substitute your name for Martha's and read that line again.

Is this true of you? Are you anxious about many things? Certainly, there's no shortage of matters to be anxious about in our broken world—health, money, job security, children, aging loved ones, the future, and the list goes on and on.

"In the multitude of my anxieties within me,
Your comforts delight my soul."
Psalm 94:19 NKJV

▶ **If You Say:** I'm afraid that my situation is impossible.

The Lord Says: I can make all things possible.

"What is impossible with man is possible with God" (Luke 18:27).

▶ **If You Say:** I'm worried that I'm not wise enough.

The Lord Says: I will give you my wisdom.

"If any of you lacks wisdom, you should ask God, who gives generously to all without finding fault, and it will be given to you" (James 1:5).

▶ **If You Say:** I'm anxious over the cares of the world.

The Lord Says: Cast all your cares on me.

"Cast your cares on the LORD and he will sustain you" (Psalm 55:22).

▶ **If You Say:** I'm overwhelmed with fear.

The Lord Says: I will give you my strength when you're afraid.

"Do not fear, for I am with you; do not be dismayed, for I am your God. I will strengthen you and help you; I will uphold you with my righteous right hand" (Isaiah 41:10).

▶ **If You Say:** I'm so worried and anxious over the wrongs I've done and I can't forgive myself.

The Lord Says: Let go of your worries and anxieties. I will forgive you.

"If we confess our sins, he is faithful and just and will forgive us our sins and purify us from all unrighteousness" (1 John 1:9).

▶ **If You Say:** I'm anxious and worried that my loved ones might leave me.

The Lord Says: Because you are my child, I will never leave you.

"The LORD himself goes before you and will be with you; he will never leave you nor forsake you. Do not be afraid; do not be discouraged" (Deuteronomy 31:8).

▶ **If You Say:** I'm anxious about dying.

The Lord Says: I will give you eternal life.

"For God so loved the world that he gave his one and only Son, that whoever believes in him shall not perish but have eternal life" (John 3:16).

▶ **If You Say:** I'm anxious and I can't rest.

The Lord Says: I will give you my rest.

"Are you tired? Worn out? Burned out on religion? Come to me. Get away with me and you'll recover your life. I'll show you how to take a real rest. Walk with me and work with me—watch how I do it. Learn the unforced rhythms of grace. I won't lay anything heavy or ill-fitting on you. Keep company with me and you'll learn to live freely and lightly" (Matthew 11:28–30 MSG).

Rebecca Carrell's Story[47]

God's grace saturates her life. She describes herself as a "joyful follower of Jesus," a loving wife and mother, and cohosts a morning talk show on a popular Christian radio broadcast in one of the largest cities in the United States. She's active in ministry, teaching Bible studies, singing in church, and on top of that, a student in seminary. Someone like her wouldn't struggle with anxiety, right?

Meet Rebecca Carrell. She battled anxiety since she was a teenager but wasn't diagnosed until age thirty. Before learning she has generalized anxiety, she thinks anxiety is primarily a spiritual problem. Growing up in her church, anxiety isn't discussed. In implicit ways, she receives the message: if you're fearful, worried, or anxious, you just need to pray more, read Scripture more, and trust God more.

In her words, "Somewhere along the way, I had bought into the 'if you had more faith' narrative that assumed depression and anxiety were always a spiritual condition born out of doubt. Medicine was God's goodness … to the physically ill, but mental struggles showed faithlessness, spinelessness, and doubt."

During one difficult battle, her anxiety feels all-consuming: "I didn't care about my children. I didn't care about my husband. I didn't care about my job … nor did I care about the Bible study I led or the worship team I sang [in] at church. I just wanted the anxiety to stop."

Though the anxiety feels overwhelming, God's grace isn't beyond her reach. The Lord's care is evident as her husband consoles her as she cries during this difficult moment. God's grace is further evident as she feels led to meet with a psychiatrist, who prescribes medication.

She finds relief through this medication, but about three years later, Rebecca tries to wean herself off of it. However, her plan doesn't work. One December day, she begins having shortness of breath. She tries to breathe deeply and "force " herself to relax but to no avail. With her heart racing, and her palms sweating, she scolds herself, saying "Stop it!" But the anxiety doesn't subside.

She calls her mom, who races over to be with her. Her mother, just like her husband, consoles her, hugging her, saying, "It's okay. I'm right here." Again, God's grace—this time through the comfort of her mother—met her anxiety. The Lord says, *"As a mother comforts her child, so will I comfort you"* (Isaiah 66:13).

A few weeks later, anxiety builds up again with her mind racing, so she goes outside for a run to work it off. After a lengthy nine-mile run, she feels relaxed and relieved. However, not even two hours pass before she begins to feel anxiety coming back. As Rebecca reports, "The nervousness coiled itself around my chest and squeezed."

Finally, Rebecca receives an epiphany. Realizing a run in the sun releases hormones that improve mood and counteract stress (dopamine and serotonin), Rebecca recognizes her anxiety has a biochemical component to it. So she schedules an appointment with her doctor who helps make sense of her anxiety. Their conversation becomes eye-opening:

"What would you do if one of your children didn't make enough insulin?" the doctor asked.

"I would make them take insulin shots."

"Why?" she asked.

"Because when the body doesn't make enough of something, you need external help."

The doctor explains, "Insulin is a hormone. So is adrenaline. So is cortisol. Your brain makes too much."

She then shows Rebecca a model of a brain, pointing to an area, saying, "This is where the brain makes serotonin and dopamine. These are neurochemicals that counteract your stress hormones. Your brain does not make enough serotonin or dopamine … Rebecca, you cannot help yourself. You did not bring this on yourself. Unless you fix your serotonin levels, you will continue to struggle."

Upon hearing this, Rebecca feels relief … followed by tears. Understanding the complex physical components of anxiety leads her to get back on medication to replace the brain chemicals she's missing. Rebecca has been managing her anxiety now for years with the help of this targeted medication. She explains,

> I look at anxiety as a clinical disorder, one that really should be diagnosed by a psychiatrist. … I struggle with the clinical kind of anxiety. It's caused by a chemical imbalance in my brain, and so that means no matter how perfect and happy and shiny the circumstances in my life are—because I don't make enough serotonin or dopamine and because I do make an abundance of adrenaline—I can't calm down. I can't stop the anxiety. So I see a psychiatrist. I take medication for it. And that really, really helps me manage the anxiety.

What clarity.

By God's grace, Rebecca also shares her struggles with others. The help she receives from doctors and medicine doesn't diminish the grace of God, but are further evidences of His grace in her life. She tells people,

> If someone says, "Well if you have enough faith, and if you pray more … the Lord will heal you." I always gently say, "Well the Lord has been very gracious in healing me. He led me to a wonderful psychiatrist." And through the common grace of good medicine, I am able to function. … So God is very much in the business of healing. Just because it's through a doctor and medicine does not make it any less remarkable.

Rebecca's story shows the importance of managing anxiety from multiple angles. Physically, she exercises, verbally she consults with doctors, and medically she takes medicine. (Medication may not be for everyone who struggles with anxiety, but discussing it with a doctor is important.)

From a mental, emotional, and spiritual standpoint—mentally, Rebecca stresses the importance of journaling our honest thoughts and filling our minds with the truth of God's Word by reading it and memorizing it. Emotionally, these practices help process thoughts and emotions by meeting them with God's truth. Spiritually, Rebecca prays regularly, shares her struggles with others, gives and receives comfort and encouragement, and stays active serving in ministry. All of these practices are God's grace to help her (and help anyone) manage anxiety and move forward with hope.

Biblically, Rebecca stresses the importance of pointing people to the character of God. Passages such as Exodus 34:6 reveal God's character: *"The Lord, the Lord, the compassionate and gracious God, slow to anger, abounding in love and faithfulness."*

The Lord is not angry when we feel anxious. Instead, God looks at us with compassion as He extends His grace to us. We can freely come to Him with whatever we feel because He is faithful to love us and will faithfully provide for our future. We can find rest and peace in His loving arms. Rebecca confidently assures us, "We can trust that everything we worry about, if or when it happens, the grace of God will meet you there."

SCRIPTURES TO MEMORIZE

On whom should I **cast all** my **anxiety**?

*"**Cast all** your **anxiety** on him because he cares for you"* (1 Peter 5:7).

If I am **not anxious about anything**, will I have **peace**, and will that peace **guard** my **heart** and my **mind**?

*"Do **not** be **anxious about anything**, but in every situation, by prayer and petition, with thanksgiving, present your requests to God. And the **peace** of God, which transcends all understanding, will **guard** your **hearts** and your **minds** in Christ Jesus"* (Philippians 4:6–7).

What can help me to **not be afraid** and **not be discouraged**?

*"Be strong and courageous. Do **not be afraid**; do **not be discouraged**, for the LORD your God will be with you wherever you go"* (Joshua 1:9).

What can bring me **joy** when **anxiety** is **great within me**?

*"When **anxiety** was **great within me**, your consolation brought me joy"* (Psalm 94:19).

Where can I find **shelter** and **rest**, who is my **refuge** and **fortress in whom I** can **trust**?

*"Whoever dwells in the **shelter** of the Most High will **rest** in the shadow of the Almighty. I will say of the LORD, 'He is my **refuge** and my **fortress**, my God, **in whom I trust**'"* (Psalm 91:1–2).

Will I be **blessed** if I **trust in the Lord** and **not fear**, but put my **confidence in Him**?

*"**Blessed** is the one who **trusts in the LORD**, whose **confidence** is **in him**. They will be like a tree planted by the water that sends out its roots by the stream. It does **not fear** when heat comes; its leaves are always green. It has no worries in a year of drought and never fails to bear fruit"* (Jeremiah 17:7–8).

How can I ask **God** to **search me**, and **know my anxious thoughts**?

*"**Search me, God**, and know my heart; test me and **know my anxious thoughts**"* (Psalm 139:23).

Who is my **refuge and strength**, an **ever-present help** in times of **trouble**?

*"God is our **refuge and strength**, an **ever-present help** in **trouble**"* (Psalm 46:1).

What does **anxiety** do to the **heart** and what **cheers it up**?

*"**Anxiety** weighs down the **heart**, but a kind word **cheers it up**"* (Proverbs 12:25).

About what **things** should I **think**?

*"Whatever is true, whatever is noble, whatever is right, whatever is pure, whatever is lovely, whatever is admirable—if anything is excellent or praiseworthy—**think about** such **things**"* (Philippians 4:8).

NOTES

1   Edmund J. Bourne, PhD, *The Anxiety & Phobia Workbook,* 6th ed. (Oakland, CA: New Harbinger Publications, Inc., 2015), 1.

2   Hannah Ritchie and Max Roser (2019), "Mental Health," 2019. Our World in Data: ourworldindata.org.

3   Carolyn Chambers Clark, ARNP, EdD, *Living Well with Anxiety: What Your Doctor Doesn't Tell You That You Need to Know* (New York, NY: HarperCollins Publishers, 2006), 11.

4   Joseph LeDoux, *Anxious: Using the Brain to Understand and Treat Fear and Anxiety* (New York, NY: Viking, 2015), 2.

5   LeDoux, *Anxious*, 2.

6   W. E. Vines, M.A., Merrill F. Unger, ThM, ThD, PhD, & Williams White, Jr., ThM, PhD, *Expository Dictionary of Biblical Words* (Nashville, TN: Thomas Nelson, 1984), 160.

7   National Institute of Mental Health (NIMH), "Anxiety Disorders." National Institute of Mental Health: nimh.nih. gov (October 9, 2019).

8   Gregory L. Jantz, PhD with Ann McMurray, *Overcoming Anxiety, Worry, and Fear* (Grand Rapids, MI: Spire/Revell, 2011), 18.

9   National Institute of Mental Health (NIMH), "Panic Disorder: When Fear Overwhelms." National Institute of Mental Health: nimh.nih.org (October 10, 2019).

10   NIMH, "Panic Disorder."

11   Archibald D. Hart, *The Anxiety Cure: You Can Find Emotional Tranquility and Wholeness* (Nashville, TN: Thomas Nelson, 1999), 9.

12   National Institute of Mental Health (NIMH), "Social Anxiety Disorder: More Than Just Shyness." National Institute of Mental Health: nimh.nih.org (October 10, 2019).

13   Stephanie Dolgoff, "Is It an Anxiety Attack or a Panic Attack?" Good Housekeeping: goodhousekeeping.com (October 11, 2019). Article link first referenced on the Anxiety and Depression Association of America (ADAA) website, https://adaa.org/node/4561.

14   National Institute of Mental Health (NIMH), "Depression." National Institute of Mental Health: nimh.nih.org (October 14, 2019).

15　Anxiety and Depression Association of America (ADAA), "Depression." Anxiety and Depression Association of America: adaa.org (October 14, 2019).

16　Hart, *The Anxiety Cure,* 6–7.

17　American Psychiatric Association, *Diagnostic and Statistical Manual of Mental Disorders*, 5th ed., text revision (Washington, D.C.: American Psychiatric Association, 2013), 189; Abigail Powers Lott, PhD, and Anais Stenson, PhD, *Types of Anxiety.* Anxiety: anxiety.org (June 17, 2019).

18　Guy Winch, PhD, "10 Crucial Differences Between Worry and Anxiety ... and Why You Need to Know the Difference." *Psychology Today: psychologytoday.com* (March 14, 2016).

19　William Backus, *The Good News about Worry* (Minneapolis, MN: Bethany House Publishers, 1991), 23-24.

20　Anxiety and Depression Association of America (ADAA), "Myths and Misconceptions about Anxiety." Anxiety and Depression Association of America: adaa.org.

21　Jonathan Davidson, M.D., and Henry Dreher, *The Anxiety Book: Developing Strength in the Face of Fear* (New York, NY: Riverhead Books, 2003), 43.

22　Gary R. Collins, *Christian Counseling: A Comprehensive Guide*. 3rd ed. (Nashville, TN: Thomas Nelson, 2007), 143–148; Bourne, *The Anxiety & Phobia Workbook*, 37–62.

23　Jennifer L. Abel, PhD, *Resistant Anxiety, Worry, & Panic: 86 Practical Treatment Strategies for Clinicians* (Eau Claire, WI: PESI Publishing & Media, 2014), 155–162.

24　Abel, *Resistant Anxiety, Worry, & Panic*, 133–154.

25　DSM-5 TR, 207.

26　For a full list of substances that can induce anxiety, see DSM-5 TR, 228–229.

27　DSM-5 TR, 189.

28　Anxiety and Depression Association of America (ADAA), "Facts" (Silver Spring, Maryland: Anxiety and Depression Association of America, 2018). Anxiety and Depression Association of America: adaa.org (October 7, 2019).

29　For more on the connection between nutrition and anxiety, see Bourne, *The Anxiety & Phobia Workbook*, 345–371.

30　Anxiety and Depression Association of America (ADAA), "Sleep Disorders," https://adaa.org/understanding-anxiety/related-illnesses/sleep-disorders (accessed August 17, 2020)

31   Bourne, *The Anxiety & Phobia Workbook*, 60.

32   Bourne, *The Anxiety & Phobia Workbook*, 40–41.

33   Bourne, *The Anxiety & Phobia Workbook*, 47–48.

34   DSM-5 TR, 189.

35   Saint Francis de Sales, *Introduction to the Devout Life*, part IV, chapter XI, "Anxiety of Mind."

36   Lawrence J. Crabb, Jr., *Understanding People: Why We Long for Relationship* (Grand Rapids, MI: Zondervan, 2013), 17–18, 124–127; Robert S. McGee, *The Search for Significance: Seeing Your True Worth through God's Eyes*, rev. ed. (Nashville, TN: Thomas Nelson, 2003), 6–11, 21–24.

37   Rhett Smith, *The Anxious Christian: Can God Use Your Anxiety for Good?* (Chicago, IL: Moody Press, 2011), 83–84.

38   Bourne, *The Anxiety & Phobia Workbook*, 91–92.

39   Bourne, *The Anxiety & Phobia Workbook*, 93–97.

40   Bourne, *The Anxiety & Phobia Workbook*, 357–358.

41   Rebecca Carrell, "Anxiety & Worry and What Not to Say." *Honest Conversations*, podcast audio, August 12, 2019, https://podcast.app/honest-conversations-heartstrong-faith-p733673/.

42   Robert P. Lightner, "Philippians" in *The Bible Knowledge Commentary: An Exposition of the Scriptures*, edited by J. F. Walvoord and R. B. Zuck (Wheaton, IL: Victor Books, 1985); Roger Ellsworth. *Opening up Philippians.* Opening Up Commentary (Leominster: Day One Publications, 2004); Richard R. Melick, *Philippians, Colossians, Philemon*, vol. 32. The New American Commentary (Nashville, TN: Broadman & Holman Publishers, 1991).

43   Bourne, *The Anxiety & Phobia Workbook*, 273–290; J. P. Moreland, *Finding Quiet: My Story of Overcoming Anxiety and the Practices That Brought Peace* (Grand Rapids, MI: Zondervan, 2019), 52–53.

44   Moreland, *Finding Quiet*, 53.

45   For more on correcting mistaken beliefs, negative thoughts, or lies, see Bourne, *The Anxiety & Phobia Workbook*, 219–236. See also Leslie Vernick and Chris Thurman, "Change in Process: Working from a Biblical Model of TRUTH in Action" in *Competent Christian Counseling: Foundations & Practice of Compassionate Soul Care*, edited by Dr. Timothy Clinton and Dr. George Ohlschlager (Colorado Springs, CO: WaterBrook Press, 2002), 372–373.

46 Adapted from *Bourne, The Anxiety & Phobia Workbook*, 226.

47 Rebecca Carrell, "When the Brain Betrays the Body." Published May 2019. *Fathom*: fathommag.com (October 22, 2019). "An Unlikely Pair: Baring Brokenness and Bearing Fruit. " Published April 19, 2019. HisAir.net (October 22, 2019). "Anxiety & Worry and What Not to Say." *Honest Conversations*, podcast audio, August 12, 2019, https://podcast.app/anxiety-worry-and-what-not-to-say-e68223090/.

HOPE FOR THE HEART TITLES

- *Adultery*
- *Aging Well*
- *Alcohol & Drug Abuse*
- *Anger*
- *Anorexia & Bulimia*
- *Anxiety*
- *Boundaries*
- *Bullying*
- *Caregiving*
- *Chronic Illness & Disability*
- *Codependency*
- *Conflict Resolution*
- *Confrontation*
- *Considering Marriage*
- *Critical Spirit*
- *Decision Making*
- *Depression*
- *Domestic Violence*
- *Dysfunctional Family*
- *Envy & Jealousy*
- *Fear*
- *Financial Freedom*
- *Forgiveness*
- *Friendship*
- *Gambling*
- *Grief*
- *Guilt*
- *Hope*
- *Loneliness*
- *Manipulation*
- *Marriage*
- *Overeating*
- *Parenting*
- *Perfectionism*
- *Procrastination*
- *Reconciliation*
- *Rejection*
- *Self-Worth*
- *Sexual Integrity*
- *Singleness*
- *Spiritual Abuse*
- *Stress*
- *Success Through Failure*
- *Suicide Prevention*
- *Trials*
- *Verbal & Emotional Abuse*
- *Victimization*
- *Worry*

www.hendricksonrose.com